Daring to dream

Reflections on the year I found myself

Daring to dream

Reflections on the year I found myself

KAREN ELY

Library of Congress Control Number: 2006908007
Publisher: A Woman's Way

ISBN 978-1-4116-9382-1
First printing, July 2006

Graphics and cover design by Thunder Mountain Design
Cover photograph by Vince Fazio
Author portrait by bcphotography.com
Photographs throughout the book by Karen Ely
Editing by Sylvia Somerville and Rebecca Anderson

For my daughters
Robin and April

The risks of not making changes are great.
We risk missing our lives.

– GAIL SHER

Contents

Introduction

This is my story . . . but in so many ways, it is every woman's story.

It is about a year in time, a year when I lived on the top of a mountain in near total
silence and found myself. It was a year of sadness and loss but, more importantly,
it was a year of incredible magic.

Daring to dream: Reflections on the year I found myself is my story of coming to grips with
a life I could no longer live and walking toward a self that I no longer knew.

Other women's stories have encouraged, empowered and inspired my life's path.
If my story can touch my daughters, other women and their daughters, then it will have
been worth the journey.

I write to tell myself the truth.

– JULIA CAMERON

PART I

Waking up

The privilege of a lifetime is being who you are.

– JOSEPH CAMPBELL

It is 4:30 in the morning, Mother's Day 1998.

I am awake and crying. The decision I have needed to make for ten years came screaming at me in the middle of the night. After years of working with women in crisis, I realize that I'm becoming one of my clients. 32 years of begging, crying, counseling and praying have failed to make an impact on my marriage. At what point do I really expect things to change?

I have to leave.

As usual, my timing stinks. Mother's Day is no time to tell my children, my husband, and MY mother that I have decided to leave my marriage and my life. The only life they know as mine. The only life I know as mine.

My husband of 32 years is sleeping quietly beside me, unaware of the huge changes looming for both of us. The implications are staggering. I am 52 years old. I have never lived alone and I have never supported myself. And my daughters . . . how do I look at them and explain that all of our dreams for the future are over? I have spent the last six years on a spiritual journey, enough of a path to know that I have only begun this excavation into me and my understanding of my place on this planet. I have glimpsed just enough to know that I'm not living comfortably with who I am. I'm afraid that if I don't leave, the me I am trying to find may disappear completely.

My decision to leave has little to do with my husband and everything to do with me. I like myself with my friends, with my children, with my family and at work. I no longer like myself with my husband. I wish there were an easier way, but I know it's often necessary to leave home in order to find answers, to find yourself, to breathe, to be able to grow. I have been (by choice) everyone's caretaker for so long that I am no longer able to let anyone care for me. "Not to worry, I'm in control and if I stop this balancing act, the entire world may stop turning." I am trying desperately to remember the sweet, innocent, loving girl of my youth. But I see only emptiness and I feel only confusion.

Like so many women, I have become everyone's expectations. Am I pretty enough? Am I thin enough? Am I a good enough _____(you put in the word . . . mother, friend, wife, daughter)? Am I enough? Will I ever be enough?

I have become someone I no longer like.

The fatigue is overwhelming.

It is so quiet here, surrounded by nothing but the majesty of the Colorado high country. It is May, a beautiful time of year in many places, but mud season in the mountains. Still, there is a faint feel of spring in the air, new birds at the feeders and little sprouts peeking out of the last-lingering snowdrifts.

At this moment, I can't imagine living anywhere else.

The serenity of my nest is being destroyed by the piles of packing materials, the stream of tears, the weight of things left unsaid, and the pain of our future disintegrating. My husband, Chris, and I have been packing for weeks. The house is sold, he has found an apartment in Colorado Springs, and yet I have been unable to say clearly what I need to say.

I am leaving.

For some unfathomable reason, he has chosen to believe what we are telling everyone else – that his work is taking him to Colorado Springs and that I will stay with a California friend until we decide where we are going to live. The fatigue of this charade is overwhelming.

Lies . . . I am so very tired of the lies.

For many years we have been living and telling half-truths. I 'm not sure when it began, but it has become a way of life. A way to keep from telling everyone the truth – that he has been unable to keep a job, that we are out of money. We must be total morons. Suddenly I'm unable to take one more step down this road of deception. I'm desperate for honesty. Will I know it when I see it?

Chris and I are finishing breakfast and preparing to head into Denver for a day of car hunting, a quiet moment of tea before the busy day ahead. Not a cloud in the beautiful sky, soft breezes and the quiet familiarity of time with someone I have awakened to for 32 years.

"I am going to file for divorce."

The quiet in the room is deafening. He must have known this was coming, but he just sits and stares at me. Nothing else is said. No fighting, no tears, no begging, just nothing. After a lifetime together, it is over in one quiet, sad moment.

Keeping myself sane.

I'm grappling with a way to be, a way to transition into a new and very different me, a different way of life. I have always lived the life I knew I would live, the life of childhood fairy tales, the life of my parents. I'm afraid that my daughters will spend years in therapy talking about their crazy mother; my parents seem to believe that I have lost my mind. Maybe I have.

My fears run rampant.

Sitting on the deck, I'm looking at a view so serene and beautiful that is seems surreal. Pike's Peak sixty miles to the south, soft quaking aspens, towering pines, and not a sign of human life in sight. I sigh and try to drink in the quiet perfection.

I'm struggling to stay focused. Few people really know what is happening. I need it this way. At the moment I'm having enough trouble keeping myself grounded and sane without caring for everyone else. It's taking a great deal of energy just to get through each day. I don't really know where to go or what to do . . . or for that matter how to act or where to live. Talk about a leap of faith, I'm beginning to believe that I may have taken a leap of insanity. A friend in California has a small trailer in her back yard, an RV with no real amenities and inside dimensions so small (she informs me gently) that I will run into myself rolling over in bed. I'm holding onto this little fantasy, hoping that it will offer me some peace and a space to find myself.

My job presents another hurdle. I love my job – running a small arts center in a little Colorado mountain town. How perfect is that? The pay worked while I was married, but will not work for a single (what a scary word) woman.

Monte, the president of the board of directors, is a kind and gentle man who lives down the mountain from us. He's an artist, completely committed to his dream of an arts center. I have to look at him and tell him I am leaving – the second director to resign from the arts center in a year.

"I have to resign and move to California."

The second man in one week to stare at me blankly. (What is this thing I have with men?) I'm not sure what he is thinking or feeling and realize that I don't know Monte very well.

Totally oblivious to the movement of the Universe, however, I think, "one more thing out of the way, one more step toward California." (Foolish woman still believing she's in control of her destiny.)

Emptiness.

I was utterly unprepared for coming home to a half-empty house. I knew my husband and a friend were moving half of our belongings to his new apartment this afternoon. Still, I'm stunned. I'm walking around a home that I no longer recognize, so many memories disappearing, so many carefully purchased furnishings are packed away and gone forever. Our home now rings of emptiness, a hollow sound bouncing off the walls, through my mind and lodging in my heart.

I begin to think I may not survive this.

I call my friend Lana, desperate for something familiar. At the sound of her voice, I quietly ask her to talk to me, just continue talking until I can breathe again. Breathe, Karen, breathe. You can do this.

I'm walking around our home, wandering from room to room, trying to take in the enormity of what is happening. A month ago my youngest daughter, April, left for graduate school; today my husband moved out and soon I will also be leaving. 32 years of marriage has come down to just this – empty walls, missing furniture, echoes of lost dreams and the realization that I am now alone.

Do I know how to be alone?

I pull myself together and decide to attend my weekly writing class in town. Once again I think I'm in control. (Oh yeah.) By the time I arrive at class, I am a joy to behold – a big pathetic ball of snot and tears.

Girlfriends have always been at the center of my life, making me laugh, sharing my joys and sorrows and keeping me sane. Even though the women in my writing class are not close friends and have no idea what is going on in my life, one look at me and they do what women do best – encourage me to tell my story. They listen intently and begin to share many of their own stories. After an hour of shared tears, I begin to feel strong enough to head back home.

However, returning to my nearly empty house overwhelms me with feelings of despondency. I am unable to eat or sleep and realize that this beautiful A-frame sanctuary is now feeling like a cold prison.

I need to move out of here soon.

How could it be over?

I cannot remember a time when my husband was not in my life. We have been friends, lovers and partners for 34 years.

Monte has kindly offered me the sanctuary of the guest suite in his home. He is the president of the arts center's board of directors, someone I hardly know, but instinctively trust. His home is quiet, he is rarely there and I'm trying to convince myself that I can find enough peace to begin to find myself and create a future.

My husband has just helped unload the last of my things at Monte's. Neither of us knows how to act or what to say. So many unkind things are being said because we are both so sad and confused. He closes the car door and backs up the steep drive, leaving me sobbing, barely able to see and trying hard to be brave and strong.

It's early spring at nearly 10,000 feet in the Colorado Rockies, a soft clear morning with wildflowers starting to bloom and a clear cloudless sky.

I am still reeling over the painful parting in the driveway when the phone rings.

My instinct is to let it ring. After all, who would want to talk to me now and who even knows where I am? Trying to compose myself, I pick up the phone and hear the soothing, loving voice of my trusted friend, Bobby. He knows me too well. I can't hide how sad and disoriented I feel. His gentle words, "talk to me," begin to take me down a path of quiet. Sitting heavily on the sofa, I am slowly transformed from a sobbing mass of insecurity and fear into some semblance of myself. Through his gentle guidance and wise words of encouragement, I hear the birds chattering for the first time that morning and begin to notice the bright sun I love so dearly. "Go outside into the beautiful mountains you love so much; they will help you feel stronger," he wisely counsels.

I begin to breathe evenly again and soon believe that I might actually survive this experience.

Hanging up after an hour's conversation and a much needed "I love you;" I am quietly wandering around the house, trying to assess my surroundings for the first time. What is his cat's name again? Is it possible for this strange place to feel like home, at least for a while? I have nothing left but a few photos and some personal items, everything else I love is in storage.

Such a long way from the fantasy in the suburbs to the quiet of this unfamiliar space.

There are few visitors here.

The early summer mornings are my favorite part of living in the Colorado mountains. The spectacular light shining through the leaves, the tall grasses and wildflowers shifting side-to-side in the soft breeze. And the smell. How can I describe the smell? So fresh, so earthy, with soft wafts of pine-scents and the incredible deep blue sky framed behind the regal pines. And a horizon stretching to the end of my dreams.

A couple of noisy jays, an occasional jet overhead and afternoon thunderboomers are all that break the tranquility. Otherwise, there is only quiet. Standing behind the house, in tall grass wet with the morning dew, I'm practicing T'ai Chi when, looking up, I'm startled to see two bull elk eyeing me warily. I am still, hoping not to startle them and wanting to etch this special moment forever in my memory. I so love the beauty of this place.

Reading voraciously, writing constantly, my journals fill with whining and angst.

Reading, writing and the quiet are slowly giving me back to me . . . one step at a time. (Well, sometimes it is one step forward, and three back.) I feel a sense of destiny, even though I don't know, or really care where it takes me. I am keenly aware that the journey is becoming my destination, and surprise myself with that thought.

My daughters are confused, my friends are struggling to make sense of my choices, and my parents . . . how can I explain all of this to my nearly eighty-year old parents? I know that I am living proof that you are never too old to make your parents crazy. It sounds selfish even to me, but I have to center all of my energy on myself for now. And so I write.

I am a writing fool.

Entire forests are being destroyed so I can write. But I have to write. I have finally taken the advice I have given to friends and clients, "write to find the truth." I sit in the yard, before the fire, in the doctor's office, in my car, at the table and in bed. But always I am writing. I am writing nothing and yet I am writing everything – the stream of consciousness that fills my journal pages often surprises me with insights and wisdom. Slowly I am carving out some truths, my truths.

And with those truths might come some peace and with some peace might come some hope.

Making sense of the difference between heart and head,

Trying to keep ego and mindless thoughts out of my journey.

"Live from your heart" I am told.

I would be enthusiastic to do just that and

Grateful if I were given the information on how to know the difference.

Then this journey would feel safe,

But safety is only an illusion and I know that peace exists only in myself.

...take a moment to tell your story

Alone.

I awake to another cloudless summer morning, alone in Monte's house.

Once again he did not come home last night, or for that matter, for the past few nights. A brief thought flits through my mind, "should I be worried about him?" But if I were worried, who would I call? Where would I look? I'm living in this man's home and yet I know so little about him. It's so strange and unsettling.

It is eerily quiet here; so peaceful at times that my chaotic mind can't seem to take it in. I had a conversation with April last night. She is struggling to understand her crazy mother. I feel so sad. How can she understand when I can't? I would do nearly anything to spare her this pain, anything, that is, except stay with her father.

I am pacing, unwilling to rest and unable to accomplish anything. Roaming from room to room, tripping over the cat and my own feet, I am feeling so alone and scared today. My parents called this morning. Mom was crying. They are so worried and so afraid that they are losing me. They don't understand what I am doing and, once again, I am unable to explain. It's taking every ounce of energy I have to get through each minute and hour of every day. And yet it seems so self-absorbed and uncaring.

I finish pacing and start to cry… again. Good God! I've done enough Buddhist reading to understand the importance of resting in uncomfortable places and breathing in the pain. I know that only through sitting, feeling and not resisting can I find freedom.

It sounds a lot easier in the books.

I need a reprieve and decide to go to the movies, something to anesthetize this overwhelming sadness. I figure that a few hours in someone else's world might make my pathetic life look better.

A drive into town and two hours of Lethal Weapon has been a total disaster. I am rushing out of the theatre, barely able to control the floodgate. Safely in my car, the tears come. I can't stop. I'm losing my mind. It's so hot and suffocating in here that I'm nearly hysterical. Can I drive? My friend Lana lives nearby. Maybe I can throw myself on her lawn; someone is bound to find me and nurse me back to some person I can remember. No.

I know that I need to feel it all.

I look in the rearview mirror. Staring back at me is the twisted face of someone I do not recognize. I marvel that no one has called 911. Doesn't anyone care anymore? I look crazy or suicidal or possibly both.

Slowly I pick up my ever-present journal and begin to write. The car is sweltering but

I don't open the windows. This cocoon of heat seems the perfect place to work through my feelings and fears. I can't see the page; but as the words begin to flow, I can feel my breath slowing. The tears begin to stop.

Some clarity and peace descend.

I am gradually able to put down my journal and look outside the car for the first time. People are coming and going, laughing, walking arm in arm. Couples, families, women and men, all caught up in their own drama.

Everything looks and feels so surreal.

. . . take a moment to tell your story

Whose life is this?

I t still doesn't feel like my life, but after several weeks, things are beginning to settle down and a new routine is emerging. Chris is visiting most weekends, mainly because neither of us knows how to continue alone. We've known no adult life without each other, 34 years as a couple heading toward a future, a future we could see and understand. This new future is much broader, but its uncharted waters leave us both faltering and confused. We can't seem to let go of each other. It's all very odd, but also comforting and familiar.

My job, my writing and reading take up a lot of my week. I am alone most of the time. The quiet forces me to go inward. I'm aware that this special time is a transformational gift. I read and connect to other women's words, their journeys, triumphs and sorrows. It helps, I am not so alone. Others have survived, but I want more than survival. At times this experience requires more strength than I feel I have.

A sudden afternoon thunderstorm gives me an excuse to stop working, turn off the computer and hang up the phone. I can feel the electricity flying around the house. At this altitude, lightning is something I've grown to respect. The blinking lights and screeching wind are rattling my nerves. The hail starts to pound out of the sky and bounce off the deck. It's now hailing so hard that I'm unable to dash outside on a flower rescue mission, all hopes of summer color dashed in a few moments.

The storm frees me from guilt. I wrap myself in a soothing blanket of words, my words and those of other women. Words are keeping me at my center, connecting me to myself, to so many women before me and too many yet to come.

I'm afraid that without the constant dogpaddling of words, I will slip under the craziness and disappear forever.

So many gifts

And yet so hard to see.

So aware

And yet so afraid.

So alive and full of joy

And yet so anxious.

So in my heart

And yet still too often in my head.

I cry how long does it take to get it right?

And yet I understand I never will.

...take a moment to tell your story

I feel so lost.

I t's late at night. I'm in bed, wrapped in my down comforter to stave off the cold of the mountain night. The quiet of the house is broken occasionally by sounds from outside. It scares me being alone in this strange house at night, lots of critter prowlers setting off motion-sensor lights and frazzling my nerves.

Looking around my room, I am reminded of a game my friends and I played as children.

"If you were to be stranded on a desert island, what would you bring?" This is certainly no desert island, but the remoteness connects me to that childhood pastime. With limited time to pack and little space here for the things I love, I scan the room quickly, making a list of what I brought to my island. Lots of photos. I love photos. Photos of my daughters, my parents, friends and family. A few pieces of wall art, my little water fountain, stereo and CD collection, desk, computer and a few personal items. Certainly a long way from several years ago, even from several weeks ago.

At times the isolation feels overwhelming, like I am lost forever.

As a heavy fog descends on the mountain this evening, I realize that I don't like fog on this mountain. It only increases my feeling of isolation. With a mountain full of miles and miles of washboard switchbacks, steep drop-offs and chiseled cliffs, this road is not for sissies. And I am definitely a sissy.

The cat dashes out from under the bed and I nearly have a heart attack. Where is Monte again? It makes me angry that he is rarely home. It's certainly not his job to take care of me and yet I feel better when he is here, just his presence makes me feel safer. At least someone might hear my screams if a bear were to drag me off into the woods.

My journal is the only constant in my life.

With my closest friends 45 miles away, my daughters and family across country, I am alone. I never thought my life would turn out this way. At 52 I believed I would have a family filled with sons-in-law and grandchildren, Sunday dinners, picnics in the park, afternoons lunching and shopping with my daughters and big family holidays.
But instead, my life has come down to just me. And silence.

But maybe we are all ultimately alone and just don't know it. I start to put these thoughts down on paper. It always calms and centers me to write and maybe I can settle down enough to sleep.

Sleep comes so slowly these days.

My world upside down.

Nothing familiar,

Nothing the same.

Changes coming by minutes, hours and days.

Coping with all the movement,

Trying to make sense of the chaos.

Working hard to stay in the moment,

Exalting in this new unfolding me

And looking forward to the person I am yet to become.

...take a moment to tell your story

Talking does not come easy.

I come from a long tradition of not talking. Well, actually, I'm not being totally honest here. I chatter constantly. I talk to friends; I talk to anyone who will listen, even sharing confidences with strangers in line at the grocery store (much to my daughters' horror over the years). But talking to people, particularly those closest to me, about emotionally charged subjects is something I seem pathetically inept at.

I come from a loving but close-mouthed family – one where personal troubles and heavy emotions were best kept inside. You certainly didn't want friends and neighbors to know you were anything short of perfect.

I've always considered myself a communicator. I was a theatre major in college and have given workshops all over the country. Why couldn't I talk to my husband and why can't I talk to my daughters? Even though it's easy to blame the demise of our marriage on my husband, I am equally responsible (and I hate that). I didn't – couldn't – speak about important issues until I was furious. And then it didn't come out well. Poor Chris just hid from my tirades and hysterics. He was used to the same scenes from a childhood with alcoholic parents. In his experience, threats were never consummated; anger always dissipated with time; and if you waited long enough, you didn't have to do a thing. And he certainly learned that one well.

God, it infuriated me – and still does!

And yet, I now realize that I didn't set clear boundaries, never drew a line of what I would tolerate or explained well what I needed and wanted. I let things slide for so long that after awhile, there was nothing left – no trust, no respect, a loss of caring and too much accumulated pain washed over the dam of our rapidly disintegrating marriage.

Except for a few close friends and my brother, I am now talking to no one about anything of importance. "Warm summer we're having, eh?" Someone please put a stake through my heart if I say one more inane thing. And yet, for the time being, I don't have the strength to answer anyone's questions or deal with their concerns.

My poor daughters. Therapists will be scribbling for years to come, "Mother is clearly the cause of all the dysfunction – obviously a disturbed and demented woman." My daughters are grasping for answers, probably burning up the phone lines gabbing about what a mess Mom is making of everyone's life. I desperately want to make them feel better, but I can't drag myself to the phone and I wouldn't know what to say when I got there.

I am unable to give them answers that I don't have.

What happens next? I'm as confused as everyone else, feeling like the center of the drain as water is sucked out of the tub and spirals down to the sewer. Does anyone

have answers to these difficult questions? Is there a book I should be studying?
I need to meditate, but first I would have to sit. And pacing is more my style these days.
Quiet, Karen. Sit quietly and breathe. The answers will come in the quiet . . . "I know,
I know . . . but I am tired of waiting and . . . really, oh so tired in general."

What do you say when you have nothing to say? Maybe that it's OK to say nothing,
to do nothing. "Just be," I tell myself. That needs to be enough for now.

...take a moment to tell your story

Menopause has been chasing me for years. It has now run me over.

The loss of periods is a joy; the hot flashes exhaust and frustrate me. Such a strange sense of humor the Universe has. Do I look like I need this NOW?

I'm awakened hourly each night, sweating, my nightshirt soaked, and then I'm chilled. Oh Joy! By morning I'm a real sight to behold, more tired than the night before and looking like something the cat threw up on the carpet. I've lost so much weight in the last few weeks that an old friend burst into tears when she saw me the other day. Between the emotional roller coaster of the separation and the loss of sleep, I have no appetite. Lord knows I could certainly use to lose some weight, but not this way.

Suddenly the Weight Watchers' plan is looking pretty good to me.

Friends and family offer wise guidance, strong shoulders and lots of laughter, staying connected to me even when I am too stressed or overwhelmed to reach out. They call, meet me for lunch and force me out of the house and into the world again.

It's all so strange, especially the familiarity.

Old haunts, past homes and neighborhoods, familiar relationships, all seem so very odd. I feel removed from everything, sort of like watching a movie I remember, but don't realize is my life. My head explodes with the contrasts, leaving me confused and unable to connect with either the old life or my new one.

As if I am not confused enough, my husband still visits nearly every weekend.

We play and relax and pretend that everything is the same, all the while knowing that nothing is as it was. Why can't we talk about what is happening? Why can't we comfort each other? We can't be there for each other because we don't know how. We have never been there for each other. Little is really new except for the sweating and physical distance between his home and mine.

Still the solitude is helping me heal.

Long hours in this slowly familiar house, working, relaxing, writing and reading. Other women's stories speak to me most; making a connection when little else does, offering comfort and direction when I feel I have lost all sense of myself. Reaching into my bedside table, I pull out my collection of index cards. Held together by a ratty old rubber band, each card represents a quote of importance to me, profound words which offer me hope and direction. As I slowly page through my well-worn cards, I begin to feel a sense of peace.

Wrapped in a blanket, cozy in front of a fire on this cool, damp night, rain falling softly outside; dusk slowly settling over the pines, I realize for the first time that I feel safe here. So strange because I know so little about the man whose house I'm living in. We've had a few late-night, soul-searching chats, but they are rare.

Mainly he works and I am quiet.

PART II

falling off course and in love

Out beyond ideas of wrongdoing and rightdoing,
there is a field. I'll meet you there.
—THE ESSENTIAL RUMI

such a strange dream I had last night, very distressing really.

Monte was in it and we were definitely more than friends. Just what we don't need, something to complicate his life and make a bigger mess of mine. What kind of unconscious mind do I have? I've never looked at Monte as more than a kind man and a friend.

Trying to put the ridiculous dream out of my mind, I bathe, dress and get ready for the day. The phone rings and it's my California friend. I'm anxious to tell her about last night's dream but when I do, her reaction surprises me. "You're in love with him. Why don't you stop trying to fix him up with all your single friends and tell him how you feel?"

I'm totally speechless. (A rare thing.)

Over the past two months I have slowly come to realize that Monte and I have an interesting connection, more like old friends getting reacquainted than mere roommates. We seem to know each other, even though we seldom talk and have always kept a respectful distance. Sort of a dance.

After all, I am still married and he is still my boss.

It's hard to believe that the summer is slipping away. I've been here since early June and yet it seems like only weeks. Months before making the decision to leave my marriage, I committed to a month-long internship at the Esalen Institute in Big Sur, a dream I had for years but had been too busy (or poor) to realize. I'm leaving my job and this house in a few weeks to head for California, first to play with friends on the Pacific coast, then to spend a month at Esalen. My friend, Carol, will drive out and spend the first 11 days with me. When I leave Esalen, I'm planning to travel the coast and find a place I can call home.

The whole prospect terrifies and excites me.

I'm energized by the ultimate adventure, heading into the unknown, all alone with nothing but a full tank of gas, a cooler of Diet Pepsi and the open road. The big sky of the west opening to embrace me and all my dreams. The deep blue sky and endless horizon to offer me hope.

Sitting on the deck sipping tea in silence, the setting summer sun wrapping me in a warm embrace, I'm thinking about my dream and trying to sort out my feelings for this quiet man. I realize that he is so respectful and gentlemanly that I have no idea how he feels about me, let alone how I feel about him.

Good heavens, I feel like a teenager, "he loves me, he loves me not."

Who cares? I am finally free for the first time in my life. What am I thinking? It has been so long since my old dating days and I wasn't good at it then. Why would I want to risk the friendship of this man? I have to get rid of these crazy thoughts, get busy doing anything but thinking about him. But . . . the thought is still out there . . . how does he feel about me? How do I feel about him?

Good grief, I am losing my mind.

. . . take a moment to tell your story

I feel like a schoolgirl.

It's a cool summer night. A crystal clear canopy of stars is spread so close overhead that it feels like I can reach out and touch it. Standing outside on this peaceful night, I am awed by its beauty.

Suddenly I feel giggly and silly. I'm standing in the driveway, arms outstretched, spinning around and around, head thrown back, watching the stars fly in circles overhead. Am I insane? Am I in love? Or are they the same thing? I cackle even louder!

There's not a house in sight so no one can see my lunacy and call the police.

Back inside, I try to make some sense out of these new feelings. It feels wonderful to feel joy again and yet isn't 52 too old to be in love? Isn't 2 ½ months way too short a time between leaving a 32-year marriage and looking at a new relationship?

I'm too smart and sensible to be thinking these crazy thoughts.

I try to read, I try to write, but my thoughts are too chaotic to focus on anything. I think back to my friend's comment, "you're in love with him." Maybe she is right. What should I do with this? The sane thing would be to keep it all to myself, save both of us a lot of potential misery and start packing for California. But I can't sleep and I'm not the type to let it go. I keep asking myself, "do I want to spend the rest of my life wondering what could have been?"

Old friends.

Monte and I sit in comfortable silence, the dinner dishes and kitchen mess awaiting our attention.

There is so much that has never been said. I'm leaving soon and I want him to know how much I appreciate his friendship, how important he has become to me, what a special man he is. I'm lost in these thoughts when he gets up to start washing the dishes. (You have to love a man like that.) We have never touched, never shared a personal confidence, but I can't leave without his knowing how I feel. I'm standing behind him when I blurt out "I love you."

He turns silently and kisses me.

After months of dancing around each other, never daring to touch, afraid of any intimacy, I feel overwhelmed by his response. Lost in his embrace, loving his touch and sweet kisses, I am swimming in warm feelings, afraid of my response and yet not wanting it to end. I didn't know it was possible to feel this way again. The night passes in a sea of gentle passion, sensual exploration and wave after wave of new experiences.

I don't want it to end; the feelings of love are overwhelming. When Monte leaves for work in the morning, I am left to savor the night, his sweet smell, his soft touch.

And to question my sanity.

I am still married, he is still my boss and I am still leaving for California in two weeks. Am I nuts? I know that rebound relationships rarely work and, after all, I'm not exactly 16.

I look in the mirror and am stunned.

I'm face-to-face with a tired-looking 52-year-old woman. It must be me but I can't reconcile feeling like a teenager and looking worse than middle-aged. I feel 30 years younger than I did just 12 hours ago. My mind is whirring blender-like, out of control with no off button. I'm not sure whether I should laugh, sigh or cry. Maybe it's menopause.

With a gasp I realize that my parents might be right – I am crazy, not at all normal.

Maybe I've jumped off the precipice of sanity and am about to splat headfirst onto the canyon floor below. Sane middle-aged married women do not behave like this. Sitting heavily on the bed, I realize that nothing has ever felt so right; nothing has ever felt so normal, so natural.

I just met this man and yet I have known him many lifetimes.

This is definitely not in my plans.

This is my time, my journey. Time to find myself, continue on my spiritual path. This detour is absolutely not in any of my Buddhist readings.

Why is it that life continues to happen despite our plans?

Days are slowly passing, moving in a slow-motion haze of lovemaking, pillow talk and laughing so hard that I fall off the bed convulsed in tears. He is funny, tender and sweet. My love for him is growing by the day.

Reality, however, is about to smack us over the head in the form of the outside world, my other life.

Chris is planning his next weekend visit and my youngest daughter, April, will be coming soon for a weeklong break from grad school. I am suddenly feeling very married, very schizophrenic and extremely confused. How can I marry this teenaged-feeling with my role as wife and mother? My relationship to my two daughters and my role as their mother is of primary importance to me. They are both confused enough by what is happening.

I wouldn't dream of throwing Monte into this soup, not for his sake, not for their sake and, most definitely, not for mine.

My Love,

I owe you so much.

You've taught me I can be loving,

You've reintroduced me to myself,

You've opened up my tired and often closed heart,

You loved me and touched me when I needed it most.

I will love you forever.

It's very clear that Chris cannot visit; I could not live with the dishonesty. April will have to spend a few days with me in town and a few nights with me at Monte's house, but I know that I cannot share this relationship with her now. There will be time enough in the future. After all, I have no frame of reference for Monte in my life, let alone how to put him in the context of hers. She is 24 years old, but she will always be my baby.

Foolish as it might seem, I feel that it's my role to protect her.

. . . take a moment to tell your story

Chris does not visit, April does.

H alf-truths, things left unsaid, uncomfortable silence. It's all too weird for words. Spinning, spinning in some pattern I cannot detect. The Universal flow is pushing me through these events, toward some future I can't envision and am afraid to imagine. I have to leave for California in a few days, and I can't even get my head together enough to do the laundry.

I know that in this chaos there lies a future but, more importantly, that there is a present.

I'm trying to relax into the now, feeling what I'm feeling and knowing that everything is as it should be. Listening to all of the Buddhist teachings in my head, I ease myself into acceptance and love, first for myself and then for others. I know that I'm creating the insanity of this situation in my head, that reality just IS – not inherently good or bad.

The past week with Monte has empowered me, helped me feel loved when I didn't feel very loveable, helped me feel strong when I felt pathetic and panicked. But my love for him is going to make it even harder to leave, for fear of hurting him and for fear of disrupting this precious time together.

I'm concentrating on breathing, one breath at a time, and being present to the magic of my life. There will be many teachers to come, many lessons to be learned and much growth to be had; but for now, I am me and this needs to be enough.

There is safety in hibernation

But little growth and creativity.

Perhaps the time is rapidly approaching to let the cloak fall,

Face my fears and approach my future.

Exciting and overwhelming but

I am up for the journey.

PART III

On the road

Inner landscapes hold the patterns of our passion and purpose.
Without knowing how to journey there, our lives remain unlived.

–DAWNA MARKOVA

I can really be ridiculous.

I like to think of myself as a photographer, not so much because I'm particularly competent, but because I think it sounds romantic.

I've always wanted to take photos of the funky mailboxes on this mountain. They are true homage to human creativity, ingeniously designed to prevent the ever-present snowplow from mowing them down. And since the plows are needed nine months a year up here, it is in truth a challenge.

So here I am. 6:00 in the morning, crawling through the damp waist-high grass, trying to get the right angle on a neighbor's mailbox, praying that no one sees me and thinks I'm insane. I laugh to myself as I line up the shot.

This whole scene is made even more ridiculous by the fact that this is one more extremely pathetic attempt to prevent me from packing.

I've had 2 ½ years to take pictures of mailboxes and I'm compelled to snap away on a day when I have a hundred items on my to-do list, all things needing to be completed before I can drive out of town early tomorrow morning. I have always believed that one of my strengths is my organizational skills, but you would never know it by the sight of my bedroom.

But at this very moment, the light is perfect and I'm compulsively snapping away rolls of film, recording tacky mailboxes for eternity. Go figure!

Back in the house, I realize that there is no point in alphabetizing Monte's spices (he has none) or in any other obsessive activity; I need to get to work. Friends and family call throughout the day, all worried about my solo trek, many afraid I might never return. Some believe that Esalen is a cult and fear that I might be brainwashed and held captive. My only fear is that I will be unable to leave <u>this</u> place.

But my adventurous spirit takes over and in a froth of activity, I begin to pull this venture together. By dinner I'm packed and sitting on the bed. My last night with Monte and he is nowhere to be seen.

Dark comes and I'm still alone.

I begin to worry about him when I hear his truck on the gravel driveway. When I finally see his face, I know what has happened. He could not come home without facing my leaving. I never wanted to hurt him.

A perfect moment.

A breath between moments really. A pause where you slip into the flow of universal rhythm, a place of magic where anything is possible.

Such was my dance with Monte.

The early morning light filtered softly through the aspens. Surrounded by tall grasses lightly covered with dew, there was no movement, not even a gentle breeze, just silence . . . and the quiet strains of George Strait's "I want to dance with you" playing on the car radio. Standing in the driveway, wrapped in each other's arms, swaying softly to the sweet rhythm, savoring our last minutes together, I know I will remember this moment forever.

How do I say goodbye to someone I cannot say goodbye to?

This sweet man means so much to me. Loving me, caring for me and giving me someone to lean on. Our time together has been so short and yet so precious. Looking into his sad eyes, I wonder about the wisdom of allowing myself to love him. The timing of this love has been so inconvenient. But is loving someone ever a decision? Is loving someone ever wrong?

I'm full of questions with no answers.

Backing slowly out of the steep mountain drive, I see him growing smaller and smaller in the distance. Dappled in the beautiful early morning light, his smile is no longer visible, only his hand waving good-bye.

Tears start to come.

I've never been a crier.

ometimes I've wished I were. It seems so female and sweetly vulnerable. However, sweet and vulnerable are not adjectives generally used to describe me. Organized, opinionated, passionate, headstrong, scrappy, funny – much more my style.

Only my soon-to-be-ex ever described me as sweet. Good God, did he know me at all?

I might not have been a crier before, but I believe I've been cured because I've been crying for months now. Driving into Denver to pick up my friend, Carol, who will accompany me on the first leg of my nearly two-month journey, the sadness lifts and I suddenly feel a rush of adrenalin. I'm really doing it. After months of planning – months filled with incredible highs, lows, fears and joys – I've stepped off another precipice. On my own. No husband, no boyfriend, no children, no one but me. What a powerful feeling!

I'm single. I'm free. I'm broke. I'm afraid.

Still, I feel high and giddy, giggling my way down the highway into Denver. With Carol and her suitcases packed safely on board, we head for Cheyenne and then on to the Pacific coast. Carol, like most of my friends and family, know nothing about my relationship with Monte and little about the details of what has happened between Chris and I. She has been gracious enough not to ask why we are separated, what Chris is doing in Colorado Springs and why on earth I'm living with a "strange" man. I'm amazed that so few people have pressed for the details that I have been unable and unwilling to share.

At the moment, I'm glad to be traveling with gentle Carol, someone who asks little and gives so much. What an incredible gift. Weeks with a dear friend, surrounded by spectacular natural beauty, wonderful conversations and laughter. The perfect ending to a difficult summer.

Better yet, the perfect new beginning.

Carol has always liked Chris.

That thought really irritates me. Yet I know I have to agree – the man can be likeable. (Like many people you don't have to live with or depend on.) Driving through the wide-open spaces of Wyoming, I am uncharacteristically quiet. I know I cannot spend nearly two weeks with Carol and not share the details of the past four months. It would not be honest and God knows I really need to talk to someone about the lunacy of these past months.

How do you start a conversation you don't really want to have?

After the year I've had, it should be getting easier, I tell myself. And yet, I hesitate. I'm afraid of the judgments (ones already running around and around in my head). "Why would you give up on a marriage of 32 years?" "How could you be involved with someone else when you aren't even divorced yet?" "Did Monte have anything to do with the ending of your marriage?" "You are obviously some sort of a slut."

Let's face it; no one can hurt us like we hurt ourselves.

"Chris and I are separated, I'm filing for divorce and because I've completely lost my mind, I have fallen in love with Monte." Sometimes you just have to say what you have to say.

I'm relieved. The judgments do not come, only support and love. Such an incredible release, one that opens a floodgate of words and feelings, fears and joys, tears and laughter. We talk and talk for hours about everything – life, love, family, friends, lust, sex, trust – as only two girlfriends can.

The miles melt away and we suddenly find ourselves in Utah looking for a motel for the night.

Tucked snuggly into bed in a mediocre (cheap) motel room that is exactly like every mediocre motel room in the country, I gently ease my journal out of my suitcase. The quiet in the room is broken only occasionally by a car door slamming in the parking lot or by the screaming of a semi on the interstate ¼ mile away. I realize with a start that this is the first time I've journaled in days, being way too caught up in the drama of being in love. Why is it that I write more frequently when I'm full of angst then when I'm full of joy? I write feverishly in an attempt to make sense out of this question. I turn out the lights when I can no longer keep my eyes open.

Another night, another motel room.

New town, same noises, same smells. Good God, even the drapes, pictures and bedspreads look disturbingly alike. Carol is asleep and I am writing.

Being in love is distracting . . . and expensive. I no longer pass a pay phone without wanting to call Monte or drive by a card shop without wanting to buy an "I love and miss you" card. It feels wonderful and worrisome at the same time. I feel lost in him, wanting to wrap myself in his love and life and fear losing mine at the same time. I have been desperately searching for me and know that I can't find that person in another, no matter how wonderful the experience.

Now I'm free and I'm no longer sure what that means.

Is Monte just another speed bump along the journey? I'm determined to stay fixed on the horizon of truth, my truth, and moving in the direction of finding out who I am, where I'm going and what in the hell it all means.

A soulful whistle in the distance breaks my train of thought and brings me back to the moment. Looking around the dingy little motel room, I'm wondering about my future. Nothing looks like it did just three months ago – no husband, no home, no furniture, nothing. Everything I own crammed into a self-storage space in Colorado. 32 years of memories covered with dust and probably melting in the cheap non-climate-controlled storage facility. Oh God, my mind is now taking me down a path I can't afford to travel. But . . . I start thinking about my girls' baby pictures in those boxes and I start to unravel.

No longer so stoic and brave, I fall asleep with quiet tears running down my cheeks.

I never knew I loved the Pacific Ocean.

Until a short trip to the central California coast this past spring, all bodies of water seemed the same – big and wet. Then I saw the Pacific Ocean and a love affair was born. The rugged coast, the soft air and exploding waves touched me in ways I still can't explain. The magic transformed me and drew me to return.

As Carol and I wind our way closer and closer to the northern California coast, we are as excited as a couple of kids at Christmas. We share a love of this beautiful ocean and can't wait to see it, smell it, feel it, walk along its shore. Barreling out of the car at the first sight of the shimmering sliver of distant blue water, we race down a steep grass-covered knoll and stop in reverent silence at our first sight of the rolling waves. Its beauty takes my breath away, its immensity demanding respect and awe.

Sitting quietly in the sand, I let the experience wash over me.

The sounds of the gulls, the rhythmic crashing of the waves, the soft breeze rustling through the tall grass. At this moment anything seems possible, all of my self-imposed restrictions and excuses melt away. There is no sadness, fear, joy or pain. Only quiet. I want to stay inside this space forever.

At the same time I understand that I'm the only thing that prevents that from being possible.

The power of the ocean

To cleanse and release.

The power of the ocean

To rejuvenate and empower.

The power of the ocean to clarify through its strength

And calm through its beauty.

The power of the ocean to inspire and give courage.

The power of the ocean as a teacher of the differences and

The giver of perspective.

The power of the ocean as the giver of truth.

The calm.

Carol and I still have 10 leisurely days together, days to walk on the beach, explore delightful little seaside towns, visit old friends and enjoy the beauty of the northern California and southern Oregon coasts.

We worked closely for so many years that our time together is effortless, comfortable in ways only possible with old friends. We can finish each other's sentences, laugh at old stories, talk about anything and everything. (She can even read my handwriting.) There is something magical about car travel – few distractions, miles of pavement and white highway noise – that creates an unreal environment, one where intimacies are easily shared.

We talk often about relationships. Hopes, fears and fantasies fill hours of our time between stops. As the miles tick away, the past drops off like unwanted layers. The weather is perfect, the time passing as a beautiful dream.

In a hotel on the Oregon coast, I pull my bed next to the open patio door. Lying in my cot, I can watch the moonlight bounce off rows of whitecaps; see the mist rolling around on the beach. Life can't get any better than this.

And yet in spite of this perfection, I can't quiet the chatter of my mind, can't relax into the beauty of the space, my thoughts go 'round and 'round in circles like the end of an old LP. I beg the endless noise to stop. (Why is it that your mind never runs reruns of the good stuff?) The negative voices just pile up higher and higher until I pray for sleep . . . or morning, whichever comes first.

Release finally comes as I fall into a deep sleep. Morning brings a misty quiet.

Carol has so much knowledge of marine biology and I'm like a sponge, asking endless questions and soaking up new information. The tidal pools present new places to explore, their miniature worlds absorbing us for hours, creating a meditative space of quiet. Sitting on the rocks, mesmerized by the ocean view, letting the sun wash over my face, I feel small, all of my problems unimportant. And yet at the same time, I feel an expansive sense of potential, a growing belief that anything is possible.

Next week Carol flies home and I will travel on alone. I suspect the coming month will provide some discomfort, but I'm also hopeful that it will provide some much needed answers.

Traveling Alone.

Are new experiences any less delightful alone than when traveling as a couple? That's certainly what the media would suggest. After all, beer commercials are not full of pathetic single people drinking and eating alone, are they?

Actually I'm not sure of anything anymore.

Carol left for home yesterday and I'm staying at a friend's house until I leave for Esalen in a few days. It's barely dawn and I'm lying in bed contemplating a day of sightseeing. I want to head to Mendocino, a little artsy town on the northern California coast. A friend suggested that I visit and see if it's a place I'd like to settle and, hooray, there's a little arts center there as well.

I am such an adventurer, loving the spirit of looking for the unexpected, poking around for hours, playing in the unknown like a kid on a summer afternoon. But I realize that I'm afraid of this adventure, that taking a trip alone might leave me feeling despondent. And I'm trying to protect myself from despondency at all costs these days.

Oh hell, what do I have to lose? I've survived despondency before. And isn't it the door to the future anyway?

Heading north on Interstate 5 and then west toward the Pacific, I feel a rising sense of joy. I have the sunroof open on my cute little white car; beautiful music playing on the tape deck and life feels good. I unexpectedly find myself in the center of a giant stand of redwoods. I pull over, stop the car and turn off the music. I am totally unprepared for what I am feeling. Sitting in the center of this nature-made cathedral, I am overcome with a sense of spiritual abundance. I lie back and take in the silence. Looking through the sun roof at thin shafts of light shooting through the forest canopy above, aiming for a place to settle on the dark forest floor below, I feel a sense of comfort, a sense of being in the presence of God. Time is suspended.

After what feels like hours, I slowly pull back onto the highway and head west toward the Pacific. I realize that traveling alone can lack a sense of shared enjoyment, but traveling companions can also serve as distractions. Would my experience in the redwoods have been the same if I had been chatting with a friend? Probably not. I realize that the experience was particularly intense because I was alone and completely present for it.

Seeing the Pacific again further lifts my spirits. God, I love this ocean, especially the northern California coast where the water explodes against the shore, shooting through tunnels in the rocks, creating a turbulent energy that excites and entrances me. Turning south toward Mendocino, I have no idea what to expect. Pulling into town, I realize that my friend was right. This is the perfect little art town. Wandering down the quaint streets that look more like New England than California, I feel myself falling in love. There is nothing not to love. Brimming with art – galleries on every corner – the town exudes a vitality that enthralls me.

Sitting in a little outdoor café, I am alone but certainly not lonely. Drinking in the soft sea air and warmed by the late summer sun, watching people moving about town, I feel a sense of home. I could live here. I wonder if there are any jobs. "I'll find the arts center before I leave town and pick up a newspaper as well," I think to myself.

Heading home through wine country, I feel drunk with happiness. Surrounded by hillside vineyards so beautiful they look unreal in the soft light of dusk, I stop to take some photos and feel completely at peace.

Today has been a wonderful adventure, a delightful day of traveling alone. It has been my first, but it certainly won't be my last.

...take a moment to tell your story

I must have a serious character flaw.

Others seem to accept things as they are, I question everything. I seem to be the only one in the room asking "why?" and "why not?"

The Esalen Institute sits in one of the most beautiful places on earth, on a peninsula jutting over the Pacific with breathtaking views and towering redwoods. Its faculty features some of the finest teachers and thinkers in the world. Coming to Esalen has been my dream.

But once again, I'm questioning everything.

I miss my home, I miss my friends, I miss my daughters. But mainly I miss being alone. Working, eating and sleeping with the same people 24 hours a day is overwhelming. I find myself obsessing over simple pleasures – like quietly sipping tea in my own kitchen – things so ordinary but now so inaccessible. This is such an unreal environment, and I'm feeling mopey and alone.

A month-long internship at Esalen includes days of working at the center. In my case this means 32 hours each week in the kitchen. The center's garden produces a wide variety of delicious organic vegetables, however, I appear to be here for broccoli season. My days are spent cutting broccoli into annoying little tree-shaped pieces.

I'm a vegetarian, but you could learn to hate vegetables here.

And then there is the cleaning. Between the smell of bleach, the mopping and the scrubbing (and the endless piles of broccoli), I'm beginning to feel sorry for myself.

Evenings and weekends are taken up with personal-growth groups. Each month's group has a different theme or direction, based on the expertise and personality of the facilitator. Our facilitator has chosen to concentrate on the Enneagram, an ancient tool for personal transformation. It includes nine personality types, each represented by a number. I have taken dozens of personality profiles. I know what the Enneagram will say. "After all, if tests are taken in the head, and not from the heart, how can they possibly provide new information," I ask myself with irritation?

I remain unconvinced.

After much self-talk (I've committed myself to a month here, what do I have to lose?) and recommitting myself to the process (Isn't this about trusting the Universe?), I decide to continue with the group.

It's clear to me that I'm a 7. 7's find everything invigorating. They are lively, spontaneous, vivacious, eager, resilient, productive and prolific. Anyone who knows me knows that I'm a 7.

After three weeks of immersion in the Enneagram, a rather reticent man in our group, Robert, approaches me and asks if I would join him for dinner. "Not a date. No expectations, only conversation. I need to talk to you." We sit at a corner table in the dining room and he begins to talk. "You see yourself as a 7 in the Ennegram but I believe you are a 2. The 2 is the most heart-centered personality in the Enneagram, and I think you're missing something valuable by not exploring it further." How annoying. He has only known me for three weeks and has never talked with me one-on-one. What is he thinking? How can he possibly believe that he knows me better than I know myself?

My world is about to turn upside down.

The next afternoon our group is offered an opportunity to participate in a Kundalini Meditation, a meditation conducted to music in four stages. The first stage standing and vibrating, the second dancing, the third sitting and the last lying down, all with eyes closed. Twelve people participate, including Robert. Standing in a beautiful white yurt overlooking the Pacific Ocean, we listen as the music begins. I move deeper and deeper into the experience, letting the music and sensations touch and move me. I vibrate, I dance, I sit and I can't stop crying. My shirt is soaked with tears, I am racked with sobs. I move into the last stage, lie down on a soft floor pillow and continue to cry.

I am a 2.

It's not clear what has happened. I have no explanation for why I know I'm a 2. I just know that it feels more right than anything I've felt in a long time. Through my tears, I struggle to make some sense out of this experience. I hug and can't let go of Robert. "Thank you, thank you so much. You've given me back to me. I can never thank you enough." For the first time in 30 years I have touched the sweet heart-centered girl of my childhood.

Back in my room that evening, I sit trying to digest the past 24 hours. I'm overcome with sadness and relief. No wonder I felt out of touch with myself, no wonder I felt so confused, so inauthentic. It feels unreal to glimpse a past I had forgotten, to touch something dreamlike within myself, to finally find a little girl who was protected for so long that I no longer knew she existed. No wonder I had to find this child.

I want to hug her and keep her safe.

I have never told my daughters that I am divorcing their father.

That decision has left us disconnected, unable to talk openly about this painful family transition. They know that their father and I are living apart, but no one speaks about the unspeakable, that we will never be the same family again.

Today's experience has left me raw but hopeful. I have unearthed a lost part of myself, something missing that I have been desperate to find for so many years. When I took the step of leaving my life four months ago, I didn't know where it would take me. After today's experience of finding a precious, lost piece of myself, I know that I have no choice but to continue on this path of self-discovery.

My daughters are grown women, both living their own lives thousands of miles away. Perhaps I needed the sanctuary of Esalen in order to place a call that no mother wants to make.

"I am going to file for divorce when I return to Colorado."

April is silent, holding back tears. I'm trying to explain, but my words are in vain, she is in too much pain to listen. I wish she were two years old and I could just hold her and tell her that everything will be okay. Instead I send her hugs from too many miles away and pray that, in time, she will be able to understand and accept my decision.

A call to my oldest daughter, Robin, provides few surprises. "I guess this call went better than your conversation with April." She is my less emotional, more pragmatic daughter, one rarely given to romantic notions of life-ever-after. "Please help your sister to understand," I choke out before hanging up.

I call Chris to tell him that I've talked with our daughters about the divorce. "Why did you do that before calling me," he asks.

"Because I already told you four months ago. You just weren't listening."

Sobbing, I try to explain about today's meditation and my discovery, about finding my lost little girl, a little heart-centered child that I don't know any more. His response, "I know that little girl," makes me cry even harder.

"But I don't."

. . .take a moment to tell your story

PART IV

Lives colliding

To close the door on pain is to miss the chance for growth.

–MAY SARTON

Wherever I go, I find myself.

Traveling 8,000 miles has left me essentially where I began nearly two months ago. Even though the beautiful coast I traveled, the month I spent at Esalen, the time I wandered through little coastal towns, the day of hiking in spectacular Yosemite National Park all filled my photo album and provided me with new friends and a distance from my old life, I slowly came back to the truth. The answers don't come in the adventure and the probing, but in the quiet.

And there are no easy answers.

Being in love has provided a distraction. Monte is waiting for me to return home, but I have no idea what or where that really is. I've not felt homesick since I was a child, but many evenings over the past two months, I've felt overwhelmed by feelings of loss, a loss of home, an unsettled sense of homesickness with no real image of home.

If I have no home, then I can't be homesick. I must just be sick.

I've missed Monte and agree that his plans to fly to California and drive me home might provide the perfect ending to my journey. Still I agonize over the decision. Is Colorado where I want to live? Do Monte and I have a future together? Do I want to be with anyone right now?

All of my anxiety flies out the window the minute I see him again. It feels so right to be in his loving arms, a future seems possible as I lose myself in his soft kisses.

However, I get more sullen and distracted the closer we get to Colorado. I can feel panic rising in my stomach, lodging in my throat, and am filled with a dread that makes me want to run and hide.

Returning to Colorado, it takes days of retreating before I can begin to call family and friends. I needed time to distill the past months' experiences and find my center before I can begin to face their endless questions and concerns. "Are you going to stay with Monte?" "I thought you were going to look for a job and home in California." " Was your trip, and particularly Esalen, everything you were looking for?"

The truth is that I don't know where I want to live or what I want to do. I have nothing but questions myself.

What to do?

Where to go?

I am so confused and so very sad.

Mainly feeling a craving for quiet,

Time alone and time with the one I love.

Or maybe just desperate for familiarity.

Looking to go home and having no idea where that is.

Just quiet and fearful and trying to be brave and trusting.

...take a moment to tell your story

I'm still legally married.

My relationship with Monte is a gift I share with few.

I'm trying hard not to involve him in my old life, especially in my connection to my children or my nearly ex-husband. It is something precious to me and obviously, since I'm still married, could be interpreted as the cause of the impending divorce.

I am busy feeling paranoid.

Perhaps remembering the terrifying words of my tarot reader the previous January, "By your birthday in October, nothing will be left of you but your compassion," and with my birthday rapidly approaching, I should have realized that I had real reason for paranoia. (Then it isn't paranoia, is it?)

But, trying hard to mend fences and hoping to have a "healthy" divorce, I accept Chris' invitation to lunch. Besides catching up on the past few months, I also advised him that I needed to deliver the divorce papers. It has been nearly six months since my words "I am going to file for divorce," but we have both been unable to face the truth and move forward. Rushing in late (as always), Chris sits down in the booth, obviously uncomfortable. Before we can order, he angrily pushes up his sleeve to show me a band-aid on his arm.

Do you know what this is? I just had an AIDS test, he snarls.

Sitting in a crowded restaurant, staring in disbelief, I listen as he tells me that one of my closest friends has shared with him every secret, every wish, every fear and every fantasy I had ever confided in her. Including my relationship with Monte. I hear just enough to know that half-truths and innuendoes have become reality in Chris' mind.

I sit staring at a man I do not know.

I'm confused and terrified. I understand his anger and confusion, but I am stunned by the accusations he is spewing. His list of my "alleged" lovers is endless and mind numbing. Good God, my daughter's elementary school principal is among them. How is it possible that he believes any of this? And why would my friend fill his head with such complete nonsense? Or has Chris built this tirade out of little pieces of gossipy misinformation and jealousy? Or is this his way of coping with being the one left behind? The cruelty of presenting this coup of information in a bustling restaurant leaves me horrified and speechless.

He has been my best friend for 34 years. My sense of loss is almost unbearable.

I stand and abruptly leave the restaurant. Driving away, my first thoughts, for some weird reason, are of Princess Diana. I now know how it feels to have your private thoughts published for others to discuss. Such incredible sadness. No anger, only tears. The anger would come later.

I will never trust anyone again.

As I sit sobbing on the couch wrapped in a warm blanket, I'm trying to absorb what has happened. I am characteristically beating myself up. "I trust too easily and share too much," I tell myself. If even half of the things he told me were true – especially the long laundry list of men I've slept with over the years – how in the world did I keep an anally neat home, cook good meals, volunteer, work, and make time for friends and my family and HIM?

God, I hate him! And her! Actually, tonight I hate everyone I've ever known. And a few I'll never meet.

The phone rings. It's a dear friend in whom I immediately confide. The phone rings again. It's my sister to whom (you guessed it.) I immediately confide. Then Monte comes home and (you guessed it again) I confide in him and sob on his shoulder. I'm a trusting person and can't seem to be anything else. Not even for an evening.

I am obviously hopeless.

I've always enjoyed the company of men. I've had close male friends all my life, something many married women do not have (or are not allowed to have). Chris always seemed comfortable with my male friends, never appearing jealous.

In fact, most of them became our friends as well. He always seemed happy that I had many close friends.

Or at least that is how it seemed.

And my girlfriend told me over and over through the years that I was her closest friend, that I was the only one who had ever believed in her and given her a chance, that we were "sisters".

Or at least that is what she said.

How do you trust again when the people closest to you violate that trust? It will not be easy to trust myself again, let alone others.

I want to send Chris and my girlfriend love and best wishes, to forgive them, even if I can't forget the experience.

However, I cannot do it today.

Who will hear me now?

Is this a lesson in silence

Or only a Universal push toward discretion?

Lessons learned the hard way.

Why so difficult to know the answers,

Especially with all the screaming in my head?

I can listen to me now.

I am the only one who knows the truth.

...take a moment to tell your story

Everything is familiar; everything is different.

I am such a joy to spend time with. I feel like I'm stuck in an old movie, actually a movie so old that it's in black and white with old, pathetic (read dead) actors and mind-numbing dialogue.

I'm fine living here on this mountain, a place I don't identify with my old life. Everything seems to work here. Then I switch the channel and find myself in my old world – everything familiar and everything different. I see my old home, I visit old friends, I have lunch in favorite haunts and go to movies in my favorite theatres. I always end up confused and crying.

Relationships have become particularly weird. I hate that. It used to be so clear – they are "our" best friends, they are "our" daughters, this is "our" old neighborhood, "our" past and "our" present. "Our" is no longer the same. Reconciling the old "our" with the new "my" is enough to make my head spin in circles.

Somehow, my mind can't reconcile the collision of these two worlds. Where is my husband, where are my daughters, where is our cat, and why is no one mowing our lawn? Good God have we let the place go, or what? But wait, this is not my life anymore. I live with a new man; I live in a new home. But I am a nesting sort of woman, someone most comfortable in her own space surrounded by things and people she loves.

Is it ever going to be possible to marry these two lives into some sort of sanity? Or am I doomed to live in a straight jacket, drooling on myself in the corner of a *One Flew Over the Cuckoo's Nest* sort of world?

Did I ever dream that leaving my marriage would be this difficult? And if I thought it would be this hard, would I have left? These are the thoughts, spinning 'round and 'round in my head until I scream at them to stop. "I don't want the old life and I'll find my way in this new world," I tell myself. I just need to be patient – God, but how can I be patient when I'm in such a hurry?

I have so many tools to help me on this path of self-discovery – spiritual teachers, mentors in books, the quiet sanctuary of my mountain home, and my spiritual belief in the purpose and importance of finding my own path. It's there. I believe it's there. It's just so dark in these scary boogey-men filled corners.

"Just sit in this dark place until the right space opens," I repeat over and over, trying to comfort myself.

A haze of nesting fills much of November.

The high country is covered with a blanket of snow, the environment quiet and the pace slow. It's easy to get lazy, forget the journaling, the reading, the meditation and the searching, in favor of snuggling in front of the fire and sipping tea. But just because I'm not aware of my personal work does not make it go away.

The Universe gets to decide when my life is working, not me.

I am still too often filled with angst, tears and the ever-present sweating. I want to know if there is a manual for how to deal with all of this. At least some sort of a quiz to let you know that you're moving in the right direction.

If so, I'm probably getting a C-.

On top of everything else, I'm slowly going broke. I'm still working at the arts center, a part-time job that is helping me on my road to pennilessness. I'm beginning to think that I need to find a job that pays me a living wage, but I have no idea where to begin.

Monte and I talk about living on the California coast together, something that thrills me, but he would have to sell his house and I'm not sure I'm ready for that kind of commitment. I don't want him to give up his life in order to follow my dreams and I'm not willing to give up my dreams and stay on this mountaintop with his.

I did not leave one man in order to get lost in another.

I am beginning to realize that I am a caretaker. No one is asking me to vacuum, cook, do laundry and run errands, but I do it anyway. Out of habit? Out of love? Or maybe it's just in the DNA. But once again, I'm losing myself and my direction. I know that I do not want to be dependent again on a man. This is his home, his life.

Where is my home? Where is my life?

Loving another is a mirror into myself,

A way of seeing me more clearly,

A way of hiding in the comfort of daily distractions.

Do I have the energy now to love another

When I barely have the foresight to see and love myself?

Or am I just hiding in familiarity to keep from moving toward the truth?

...take a moment to tell your story

Christmas is looming.

I can't think about the holidays. I've always enjoyed our family's traditions, traditions created by my mother and by her mother before her. Traditions based on a love of home and family. Homemade cookies, carols, decorating the house, putting up the tree, wrapping the presents, our fondue dinner on Christmas Eve, the joy of gift giving on Christmas morning. These speak of the past, of the only holiday memories we've ever known.

No one knows what to do with Christmas this year.

Christmas is not a holiday that Monte enjoys; he has too many difficult childhood memories associated with it. I want to decorate a tree and bake. He is uncommunicative and quiet. I want music and friends, food and family. He doesn't know what he wants. I have only the quiet of this mountaintop home; Monte continues to work long days, seven days a week.

My oldest daughter, Robin, and her husband are living and teaching in Mexico City. She calls and suggests that the family might best be served by throwing out the old traditions and creating new ones. Friends who live in their apartment building will be gone for the holidays so she suggests that April, Chris and I visit and stay in their apartment. One big happy family.

My friends are appalled. I should have listened.

We all arrive safely in Mexico City, trying to act jovial, like nothing has changed. But Chris is different. It was subtle at first. But hurtful little digs keep coming, piling up day after day. I reel with sadness, frustration and anger. He has a new girlfriend (he casually lets me know), wears strange clothes (sexy boxer shorts and black silk shirts?), and makes off-color jokes (I can't believe what I'm hearing).

He has become someone I hardly recognize.

For days Chris parades his liberated new life in front of me. I can hardly breathe. So many times in the past 10 years I've begged him to make a new life with me, to put some energy and focus into a marriage that was dying . . . not for lack of love but for lack of caring.

The situation becomes unbearable. There is no jolly in the Christmas of 1998, only tears.

Chris and I are fighting, saying unkind and hurtful things. April is distraught, Robin is trying to help. Robin's husband is staying out of the fray.

Sitting in bed with a flashlight late on Christmas Eve, I am feverishly looking through the phone book (in Spanish – what am I thinking?). I'm desperate to find a cab. I have to find my way home.

Will this pain ever end?

Great feelings of sadness and a sense of loss and failure overwhelm me.

I am in a black tunnel that has no end.

There must be some light in my future or else

Why would I want to continue?

God, the answers are slow and my progress seems nonexistent.

I am in a hurry for answers and a sense of direction, but

I already know the truth and there is no destination.

I need the joy, and I know I need to work through the pain.

Why so much sadness when all I seek is light?

Every family has a holiday to remember.

It will probably take years (and a great deal of therapy) for some of the images, sadness, insanity and accusations to dim for all of us. For now we can be content that no one was hospitalized, no one was murdered, and we will all (probably) recover. . . some day.

We part and I have higher hopes for 1999.

. . .take a moment to tell your story

PART V

Recommitment

Tell me, what is it you plan to do with your one wild and precious life?

– MARY OLIVER

Hibernating.

Everyone on the mountain has stored plenty of wood for the long winter nights and is prepared to hunker down till spring. I'm not fond of snow, but I've learned to love its quiet. Even the noisy chatter of the warm-weather critters goes silent, the blanket of snow on the ground, trees and grass gently quieting the noise of the world.

I'm a suburban girl. I've never wanted the "house on the prairie" life. Getting up in the morning to a freezing house, dragging fire wood from the back porch and building a fire before I can start my oatmeal makes me crazy. I begin to dream of having natural gas heat again – a life where I can push the thermostat up and magically feel instant warmth. I am restless and irritable.

I have to get serious about finding a job.

The focus of my search is centered on the central and northern California coast, but I'm trying to be open to any interesting opportunity. Monte has his house on the market and we're getting serious about looking for a life together, a place for us to start over. Are we doing the right thing? Are we doing this for the right reasons? I continue to search for insight and direction.

Pulling inside myself with no understanding of why.

Changes swirling 'round me and yet all seeming so much the same.

My world feels so overwhelming that I crave only peace and quiet

And my love to hold me.

Knowing the answers aren't in him, but in myself

And so afraid I'll never find that self again.

An opportunity presents itself to visit an astrologer. Heaven knows, I don't have extra money to spend and as I prepare to leave for my appointment, a little inner critic chimes in with, "This is a ridiculous waste of money, you irresponsible nitwit."

I go anyway.

I leave my two-hour appointment a believer. Her reading is so mind blowingly right-on that I begin to believe this coming year is not going to unfold as we are hoping. She sees Monte and a couple of friends moving to California, but she sees me moving elsewhere. This seems incomprehensible to me, but I'm trying to be open to any intuitive direction. She also sees me marrying again. (Just what I need – another husband!)

When I share this news with Monte, he looks at me like I'm a bit crazed. He doesn't really believe in astrology, even though he is trying hard to support me. I cannot imagine how the future is going to unfold but I believe in watching and listening. I have learned that forcing my will on the Universe only leads to pain and frustration. I'm reminded of a t-shirt a friend gave me years ago:

When one door closes, another opens. It's the hallways that are a bitch.

Once again I am groping along a dark hallway, hoping to find light under a distant door.

...take a moment to tell your story

A circle of strength.

I

am sitting in the middle of more memories than I feel my heart can hold.

Looking around my bedroom, I see clearly what I have felt for a long time – that I have created a cocoon of nourishment in this once strange space, a cocoon that makes me feel safe, that cradles and soothes me and gives me strength and direction.

While I am growing, my world has gotten smaller.

I can survey all the things that mean the most to me while sitting propped in my bed. I notice so many things I love and cherish – my CD player, always softly playing gentle, loving music; my little fountain, happily gurgling in the corner; a candle softly burning by my side; and photos, lots and lots of photos. Of my children, my family, my closest friends. Over my bed are several photos that include me – a bright sunny smile, arms wrapped around a loved one, all taken when I was a very different person in a very different place.

Many of my beloved quotes are framed, sitting in places I look at every day. Their wise counsel keeps my mind where I want it – focused on my spiritual path toward myself. They never let me stray far from my goal without jerking me back to the truth.

My bedside table is piled high with books – stories of other women who have grown through adversity, tales of spiritual awakening, and chronicles of hope – that I read, reread, underline, earmark and highlight. They push my one foot in front of the other, often dragging me into a self I so dearly want to find and know.

My 3 x 5 cards sit next to me, so quiet, and yet so powerful. Their hand scribbled quotes taken from so many books over too many years. A ratty rubber band barely holds them together, so rotten that it is tied together in three places. Still they sit as a mirror for me, a mirror of where I am today and a passage to my tomorrow.

This is a woman's space. My space. That thought makes me smile and sigh and dare to dream.

No one wants me.

No one is begging me to work for them, however, I'm not easily discouraged. When a writer from Mendocino (one of my first choices for a place to live on the coast) advertises for an assistant, I respond and quickly fly to California for an interview. I have only been to Mendocino in the early fall when It's fabulous; it's now February, the rain is coming down in blinding sheets and everything is flooding. It is damp and I am cranky.

I love the sun. I begin to rethink my direction.

I'm back to "he loves me, I love him." I realize that he is not my answer as I am not his. Whether or not I love him is incidental.

I have been back from my Pacific coast trip for four months and still have no leads and no direction. It's hard to keep from getting discouraged. I sit by the fire and in my room, my music playing softly, a candle flickering in the stillness while the wind howls outside, my ever-present pen and journal my constant companions.

I sit listening for guidance.

I am filled with my love for you.

Your sweet self, your cute smile, your teasing and loving ways

All make up the person whose life is so entwined with mine.

A giving and loving and safe place to grow stronger and find me.

Will this strength move me in directions alone?

Or turn inward and provide fertile ground for our love to grow?

So much good, so much sweetness and so nourishing, but

My mind can never leave anything alone.

Am I insane to fret over such a loving place till I destroy it?

Is it crazy to question everyone and everything

Or is it simply my nature?

And should it even matter?

Some day I will simply accept and love myself as I am

Some day I will simply accept and love others as they are.

If I were afraid of nothing, what would I become?

I am independent to a fault. It's not one of my most charming qualities and proves to be quite a challenge to anyone who loves me. When I moved into Monte's house, I was a quivering mass of insecurity, looking for quiet and a place to regroup. Over the past months I have slowly gotten my bearings and begun to return to my passionate, opinionated, headstrong self. Poor man. He thought he found a sweet thing, only to find me.

As I venture more and more into Denver to play with friends, travel around the state to job interviews and send resumes all over the country, Monte is feeling confused and left out. I am mainly irritated. I love him, but I'm no longer willing to be an old-fashioned girlfriend or wife. I'm really looking for a relationship to no one but myself.

If I were afraid of nothing, what would I become? I often challenge myself with "what is the worst that could happen?" My mind can conjure up horrors, but I know they rarely occur. My parents are urging me to "come home" to Cleveland, Ohio, a place where I haven't lived since I was 17 years old. I try to explain that Cleveland is their home; it's not my home. Even though I love and enjoy my family, I could never leave the west. It's a soul place for me, a place of dreams and possibilities. Without it, I could not breathe.

Freedom is on my mind.

Often I cannot see it or find it.

Why, I do not know, because it is as near as my breath.

It is in the quiet.

It is in the letting go.

It is in my heart and soul when I pause long enough to listen.

The mind chatter keeps me hostage from myself.

Letting go is the answer.

I adored my grandmother. I still miss her, even though she has been gone for more than 10 years. I always hoped she'd visit from wherever she was, but over the years I had given up hope. On a long drive home late one evening, I felt her spirit in my car. She said nothing. Her visit was perfectly timed. When I needed her most, she was there. I talked to her, crying and asking for advice, hoping for some direction and support. "Grandma, tell me what to do." That night we spoke in a dream.

"Follow your heart and your dreams."

What does that mean?

"Just what I said."

Is it in Cleveland?

"How does that feel?"

Loving, safe, caring, and boring – I'm afraid I'll be going back.

Can I make a life there?

"Can you?"

I believe so.

"See what the Universe provides."

...take a moment to tell your story

I will always call Colorado home.

I have loved Colorado since my first glimpse of the Rocky Mountains. Even though twenty years have passed since that day, I can still feel the thrill at seeing their immensity and beauty, knowing in my heart and soul that I was home. The sense of space, the colors, the feel of the air, the incredible sky, have all become so much a part of me that I can no longer imagine living anywhere else.

And yet I have a nagging sense that my future is calling me elsewhere.

March in the Colorado high country, a place of cold and snow, plows and mud. Spring is still months away and I am crazy with isolation. Sitting at the kitchen table, looking out over the frozen landscape, I see little hope of sprouts, wildflowers, soft breezes or warmth. Only cold.

I love poetry. But I'm no poet. I have long admired those who could put their words together with such beauty and clarity that I was touched, challenged and changed. I never wrote a poem in my life until last October. Sitting on my bed late one night at Esalen, poems began to come, first sporadically, then at terrifying speeds, often as many as ten in one evening. They seemed to be messages from my soul, not for anyone else, only for me. Being obedient, I listened. I wrote them down and I showed them to no one.

Stuck between two worlds –

The known and the unknown,

The scary and the scarier,

Static and freedom,

Smothered and creative,

Chaos and peace.

But only in working through the pain

Can peace be discovered.

Slowly over the past two months, I have shared a couple of poems with close friends, not knowing if the poetry was of any use to anyone and hoping that they weren't embarrassingly awful. The content is painfully personal, often coming at times of great anguish. Chris has been asking me for months to share some of my poetry with him. Because he has always been supportive of my writing, I e-mailed him several favorites and waited for his reply. Days later I learned another painful lesson.

Another lesson of trust and betrayal.

The poems did not go to him but instead went to his girlfriend's e-mail account. I didn't know he still had a girlfriend and I have no idea if she read them. But having my poems in her computer makes me crazy. I feel exposed and violated. I call him, ranting like a mad woman. He struggles to explain but nothing helps. He is quietly apologetic.

God, I hate the insanity of divorce. It started out so civil, so friendly. I had hoped we could create a new family dynamic, separate but loving and supportive, providing a space of compassion and a future of caring for each other and our daughters.

I now have little hope for a future of any kind together.

Facing myself with clarity.

Filled with excitement and terror.

How can it be that we are all alone?

Returning to the familiar –

To relationships

To daily rituals

And forgetting the truth.

My soul's journey is all that matters.

In the end I am alone with myself.

I will soon be single.

I have no idea what that means. The last time I was single I was just a child getting married, barely twenty years old, with no sense of being single. After all, children are all single. I have never known a time in my life when I wanted to be single. Growing up, my future always included a husband and children. My children are grown and gone. I soon will have no husband.

Do I exist?

And if so, how will that look? I'm now nine months (odd, the gestation period) into a search for myself, my single self. No one left to define myself by, no one left to create a home for, no one to call if I'm going to be late, no one to comfort me when I'm sad or afraid. I have defined myself by my relationship with others – I am daughter, I am friend, I am wife, I am mother, I am non-profit director – but without those definitions, who is Karen?

I know I have a self, one that existed before I burst from the womb.

I know that woman. She exists because I have seen her, I have felt her, I know her. I am searching for a way to live confidently in that space and have no idea how to do it. The truth is becoming inescapable – I must go forward alone.

PART VI

Leaving home

When I let go of what I am, I become what I might be.

–LAO TZU

saying good-bye.

My divorce papers are signed. I am single. I have no idea where this life will take me, but I know that I cannot find what I'm looking for with another person. The passage is too personal; it must be traveled alone. There is no room on this journey for the compromises required of a committed relationship.

Flying is freedom,

The open door to the soul.

Connecting my self with my Self,

Soaring vast distance without interference

And knowing I am true to my path.

A sense of exhilaration and adventure

Intermingle with fear.

No greater journey can be found than the one into myself.

Looking back over my life, I see that relationships are a dance. Something beautiful, difficult, awkward or graceful, but a dance created together, a way of being and a way of presenting to the world. My dance with Chris was filled with everything beautiful and many things difficult, but one where I was in the lead and he was too often the child. I am stunned to realize that my dance with Monte has proved to be vastly different, one where I was often the child and he was in control, I was the silly one, he was in the lead.

If I appear as two different people in two different relationships, than who is Karen?

Monte's house is sold. Temporarily he will be moving into a neighbor's home. Two friends are talking about relocating to California with him. Neither of them is me. He has been a constant in my life this past year, allowing me to lean on him, providing wise guidance and gentle love.

He says, "I know you needed time alone, but I thought you'd already done that." I know he doesn't understand but after 32 years of marriage, 6 ½ weeks wandering the California coast might be enough for others, but it's not enough for me. I love him but I cannot stay.

My job search continues in an unexpected direction.

A small ad for the director of a no-kill animal shelter in Flagstaff, Arizona catches my attention. I've been to Flagstaff. I think I could live there. I've never thought about Arizona but Flagstaff looks a lot like Colorado and its not too far. My resume goes into the mail. After two weeks, it's returned "addressee unknown." I throw it on my desk, thinking it was a ridiculous idea to begin with; after all, I know nothing about running an animal shelter.

But the letter sits and seems to beg me to do something. One day I call information, get the organization's phone number and call. A board member answers the phone, apologizes profusely saying, "They printed the wrong address in the paper. If you can fax another resume, the search committee is meeting tonight." I fax my resume, all the while thinking "dumb idea."

Why would I move to Arizona? What in the world do I know about animal shelters?

...take a moment to tell your story

Few words.

Monte is moving to his temporary residence next week and they want me in Flagstaff for a job interview at the same time. He's frustrated because he needs my help; I'm feeling guilty because I wish I could be here. But I desperately need a job and a home and I can't afford to pass up this opportunity.

History seems to be repeating itself.

I'm taken back to eleven months ago when I was leaving Chris, boxes filling our home and lots of unsaid words taking up the empty spaces. Once again, there are few words and lots of sadness.

I get on a plane.

Spending the night with old friends in Phoenix allows me to get my bearings. Nothing seems chaotic now that I have distance. With space to breathe and think, everything makes more sense. I had forgotten how much I love the desert. Arriving at dusk, the sunset takes my breath away, the entire sky running the gamut of red and orange to aqua, deep blue and black. The same magnificent sky I love in Colorado, but without the cold and snow. Sipping tea next to their pool, I begin to think that Arizona might be a place I could live.

The interview in Flagstaff proves interesting. I know nothing about their business, but I do know a lot about running a non-profit. I'm no animal expert but, then, at this point they have no animals. And I can learn. I leave the next morning believing I have the job.

Returning in the middle of Monte's move, I'm met with stony silence. I don't blame him. There is really no one to blame. And, damn it, it's May and it's snowing. This must be a sign from the Universe. I pray they offer me the job in Flagstaff because I can't imagine living on this mountain another month. What kind of place has snow in May?

They offer me the job and I begin packing.

Strange life.

Stranger course of events

Not sure what to think but struggling with direction and

Afraid to hope.

Afraid to go into the world alone.

Afraid to leave what I am comfortable with.

Afraid to leave the man I love

Afraid I will lose an important connection to my children.

Afraid I am making a huge mistake

But more excited than I have ever been.

No matter what happens,

I am free.

Free to be me.

...take a moment to tell your story

Few people like me right now.

Many people love Monte and at this moment none of them like me very much. After all, this is his life and I am the interloper. He is a sweet man and I am leaving him. The women are all secretly in love with him and he loves me. I go about my daily rituals, packing and putting my old life in order, avoiding many people, and silently passing Monte in the hall.

Once again, I think "love isn't supposed to be this way."

Neither of us is sure how to behave so everything is cordial, like strangers instead of friends and lovers. I want to hold him. I want him to hold me. He might want the same but we don't touch, we are silent. I have no idea how to move myself cross-country, having always had a husband to help, to provide some physical strength where I have little. I call my brother, Richard, and ask if he can help, but still hold out hope that Monte will be willing. I know I have no right to ask – he has already done so much.

When Monte agrees to help me move, I'm incredibly touched. It will be easier to move forward with his love and blessing. I begin to pack in earnest.

I know two people in Arizona and they both live 140 miles from Flagstaff. I love adventure but even I think I've gone mad this time.

What gifts do I have?

What direction will they take me?

52 years of age and just now really beginning to ask questions.

32 years as a wife and a mother

Allowing those positions to define who I was and what I did.

"Now what" I ask.

For the first time in my life the whole world is opening.

Yearning for adventure and afraid to venture out,

Knowing I have talent that I have just begun to tap,

Excited to find my old self so long lost and yet

Yearning for the self that I don't even know.

You're going where? To do what?

Friends and family are stunned to hear that I'm moving to Arizona to manage a no-kill animal shelter. And they're right; I certainly know nothing about it. But whether it makes sense or not, it just feels right.

I'm trying to sit quietly in this space that scares me to death.

And it isn't easy. As if that isn't difficult enough, well-meaning friends and family are ever vigilante in expressing their concerns. "Will you have benefits?" "Are you saving for retirement – you're no longer young, you know (now, that's helpful!)?" "You don't know anyone in Flagstaff. What will you do if you get sick?"

I'm sitting quietly is what I'm doing. And trying to drown out all the voices, the voices of those who love me. Inside I'm screaming, "I'm desperate for the sound of my own voice!"

If I write to sort things out and to tell myself the truth,

What am I hearing?

A mixture of fear, yearning and excitement.

I need to rid myself of fear in order to feel excitement,

To let go and let be,

To live in love and experience the world,

To be in peace and live in quiet,

To be myself and not what others think I should be.

To grow and become,

To learn and to be.

It is in that space that I'll find me.

Spring has finally arrived. The air is soft and little green sprouts are popping up and out everywhere, the frogs are chirping by the pond and the air is alive with the sound of happy critters again. I lay in bed in the early morning and listen to the symphony, not a human sound anywhere, only the beauty of nature. It is hard to imagine leaving a place I love so deeply.

But the U-Haul is filled and waiting . . . and so is the rest of my life.

Where I thought a light went out, now a candle shines.

– MARY CHAPIN CARPENTER

...take a moment to tell your story

Acknowledgements

It's a rare gift to have a year to step back from your life.

It certainly was a year to remember. I never cried so much or grew so much, read so much or wrote so much, was alone so often or in love so deeply. I don't want to forget a single minute of the experience. (Well, maybe a few.)

A year to assess where you want to go and what you want to be, to feel surrounded by love and support, to live in such a spectacular place, to have so much time to discover yourself.

I owe so much to so many.

> *My father, who always encouraged and loved me even when he didn't understand*
> *My brother, Richard, who never left my side*
> *Bobby, my spiritual guide, without whom I wouldn't be who I am*
> *Monte, who loved me enough to help me leave*
> *My mother, who loved me no matter what*
> *My girlfriends, who made me laugh and never gave up on me*
> *Sylvia, Lee and Bobby who believed in this project*
> *Dorothy, who encouraged me to take the time to complete it*
> *My daughters, who I hope never give up on finding themselves*

Without the gift of this past year, I would never have found myself.

And that is the greatest gift of all.

Karen Ely's professional life has been spent in non-profit management. From domestic violence and sexual assault to drug prevention and welfare-to-work, Karen has helped assist thousands of women through difficult life transitions.

In 2003, Karen fulfilled a lifelong dream of creating a women's spiritual retreat program. Located in Sedona, Arizona, A Woman's Way is her latest project in a life filled with commitment to issues affecting women.

It is Karen's hope that this book and A Woman's Way will benefit women searching for a spiritual center and a path back to themselves, for she believes it is the ultimate journey.

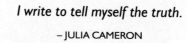

I write to tell myself the truth.

– JULIA CAMERON

...take a moment to tell your truth